A
MONTH
of PRAYER
WITH ST. FRANCIS OF ASSISI

A
MONTH
of PRAYER
WITH ST. FRANCIS OF ASSISI

Wyatt North
BOOKS THAT INSPIRE

INTRODUCTION

As much as any of the saints, Saint Francis of Assisi—born Giovanni di Pietro di Bernardone—is known for his profound piety. He is especially remembered for how he renounced worldly possessions in order to focus on spiritual things. At great personal risk, he attempted to convert the Sultan in Egypt to end the Crusades. His Franciscan Order grew quickly in his time and has since birthed several other orders that persist to this day. He is known particularly for his love of the Eucharist. According to tradition, he received the stigmata while in prayer in 1224, making him the first recorded saint to receive this blessing.

DAY 1

S t. Francis placed a great deal of emphasis on the Eucharist in his discussions of the Christian life. How can one draw near to the Lord without receiving with awe and gratitude the very means, ordained by Christ, that He has instituted as His way of drawing near to us? Thus, St. Francis goes to great lengths in his writings to reinforce the proper posture and awe a Christian should have when taking the Eucharistic host. While many people seek God in many and various places, in the Eucharist, God seeks us, He comes to us on His terms, and therefore, it is the one place where we can be certain that we are genuinely encountering the Lord.

Meditations from St. Francis

The Lord Jesus said to His disciples: "I am the Way, and the Truth, and the Life. No man cometh to the Father, but by Me. If you had known Me you would, without doubt, have known My Father also: and from henceforth you shall know Him, and you have seen Him. Philip saith to Him: Lord, show us the Father, and it is enough for us. Jesus saith to him: Have I been so long a time with you and have you not known Me? Philip, he that seeth Me seeth [My] Father also. How sayest thou, Shew us the Father?" The Father "inhabiteth light inaccessible," and "God is a spirit," and "no man hath seen God at any time." Because God is a spirit, therefore it is only by the spirit He can be seen, for "it is the spirit that quickeneth;

the flesh profiteth nothing." For neither is the Son, inasmuch as He is equal to the Father, seen by any one other than by the Father, other than by the Holy Ghost. Wherefore, all those who saw the Lord Jesus Christ according to humanity and did not see and believe according to the Spirit and the Divinity, that He was the Son of God, were condemned. In like manner, all those who behold the Sacrament of the Body of Christ which is sanctified by the word of the Lord upon the altar by the hands of the priest in the form of bread and wine, and who do not see and believe according to the Spirit and Divinity that It is really the most holy Body and Blood of our Lord Jesus Christ, are condemned, He the Most High having declared it when He said, "This is My Body, and the Blood of the New Testament," and "he that eateth My Flesh and drinkety My Blood hath everlasting life."

Wherefore [he who has] the Spirit of the Lord which dwells in His faithful, he it is who receives the most holy Body and Blood of the Lord: all others who do not have this same Spirit and who presume to receive Him, eat and drink judgment to themselves. Wherefore, "O ye sons of men, how long will you be dull of heart?" Why will you not know the truth and "believe in the Son of God?" Behold daily He humbles Himself as when from His "royal throne" He came into the womb of the Virgin; daily He Himself comes to us with like humility; daily He descends from the bosom of His Father upon the altar in the hands of the priest. And as He appeared in true flesh to the Holy Apostles, so now He shows Himself to us in the sacred Bread; and as they by means of their fleshly eyes saw only His flesh, yet contemplating Him with their spiritual eyes, believed Him to be God, so we, seeing bread and wine with bodily eyes, see and firmly believe it to be His most holy Body and true and living Blood. And in this way our Lord is ever with His faithful, as He Himself says: "Behold I am with you all days, even to the consummation of the world."

St. Francis of Assisi. *Of the Lord's Body.*

Additional Biblical Reflections: Matthew 28:29–20; John 14:6; 1 Corinthians 11:29.

Prayer

Lord, while we see the accidents of bread and wine, you nonetheless have chosen these crude vessels to become your body and blood, your presence. Let us receive the sacrament worthily and regularly, with proper contrition, so that by discerning your body, we might receive this gift to our glory and yours. Amen.

DAY 2

Today's meditation addresses two of Jesus's most difficult teachings. First, St. Francis speaks of renouncing the material world and possessions since such things can easily become false gods. Second, he urges that one love even those who might persecute them on account of their faithful obedience. This is why he argues that one should not abandon their superiors or people who are in authority, even if situations demand, for the sake of their soul, necessary disobedience. It is better to disobey and accept the consequences—if such disobedience is rooted in higher fidelity to God—than to disobey and flee.

Meditations from St. Francis

The Lord says in the Gospel: he "that doth not renounce all that he possesseth cannot be" a "disciple" and "he that will save his life, shall lose it." That man leaves all he possesses and loses his body and his soul who abandons himself wholly to obedience in the hands of his superior, and whatever he does and says—provided he himself knows that what he does is good and not contrary to his [the superior's] will—is true obedience. And if at times a subject sees things which would be better or more useful to his soul than those which the superior commands him, let him sacrifice his will to God, let him strive to fulfil the work enjoined by the superior. This is true and charitable obedience which is pleasing to God and to one's neighbor.

4

If, however, a superior command anything to a subject that is against his soul it is permissible for him to disobey, but he must not leave him [the superior], and if in consequence he suffer persecution from some, he should love them the more for God's sake. For he who would rather suffer persecution than wish to be separated from his brethren, truly abides in perfect obedience because he lays down his life for his brothers. For there are many religious who, under pretext of seeing better things than those which their superiors command, look back and return to the vomit of their own will. These are homicides and by their bad example cause the loss of many souls.

> St. Francis of Assisi. *Of Perfect and Imperfect Obedience.*

Additional Biblical Reflections: Matthew 6:19–21; Acts 5:29; Romans 13:1–14; 1 Timothy 6:17–19.

Prayer

Lord, perfect obedience often requires we walk a tightrope between both requiring material goods to survive and worshipping them, between obeying authorities and remaining faithful to what is required of the soul. Grant us the wisdom to walk this narrow path so that we might always move constantly according to your will. Amen.

DAY 3

Today's reflection is sobering. While humankind was granted more by God from the beginning than any creature, no creature has turned against God more violently and persistently. Even the demons, St. Francis points out, were never so bold as to crucify the Lord. But the answer to this devilish side of man is not in the will but the cross. Thus, if we are to take glory or refuge in anything, it must and can only be the cross.

Meditations from St. Francis

Consider, O man, how great the excellence in which the Lord has placed you because He has created and formed you to the image of His beloved Son according to the body and to His own likeness according to the spirit. And all the creatures that are under heaven serve and know and obey their Creator in their own way better than you. And even the demons did not crucify Him, but you together with them crucified Him and still crucify Him by taking delight in vices and sins. Wherefore then can you glory For if you were so clever and wise that you possessed all science, and if you knew how to interpret every form of language and to investigate heavenly things minutely, you could not glory in all this, because one demon has known more of heavenly things and still knows more of earthly things than all men, although there may be some man who has received from the Lord a special knowledge of sovereign wisdom. In like manner, if you were handsomer and richer than all others, and even if you could work wonders and put the demons to flight, all these things are hurtful to you and in nowise belong to you, and in them you cannot glory; that, however, in which we may glory is in our infirmities, and in bearing daily the holy cross of our Lord Jesus Christ.

St. Francis of Assisi.
*That No One Should
Glory Save in the Cross of
the Lord.*

Additional Biblical Reflections: Jeremiah 17:9; Romans 7:18; Ephesians 2:1–3.

Prayer

Lord, we have so often been faithless, but you have been faithful. While we do not deserve your favor, in your grace, you've come to us through the very violence we did to you and used your cross as an instrument of our redemption. Let the cross be the object of our glory so that we might not return to the ways of the flesh but would evermore be molded after the image of your Son. Amen.

DAY 4

Nothing thwarts vice better than virtue. However, as St. Francis reminds us today, not a single virtue can be apprehended by humankind lest one first dies to the flesh. That is to say; he pursues the way of the cross. Virtue is not a habit we inculcate through self-will and discipline, but we receive virtues as gifts from God, who uses both will and discipline as a farmer who waters his crops. In such an instance, it is water that undoubtedly produces a harvest but only water as the farmer gives it. Likewise, discipline alone does not produce virtue, but when proportioned according to God's goodness, a harvest of virtue results.

Meditations from St. Francis

Hail, queen wisdom! May the Lord save thee with thy sister holy pure simplicity! O Lady, holy poverty, may the Lord save thee with thy sister holy humility! O Lady, holy charity, may the Lord save thee with thy sister holy obedience! O all ye most holy virtues, may the Lord, from whom you proceed and come, save you! There is absolutely no man in the whole world who can possess one among you unless he first die. He who possesses one and does not offend the others, possesses all; and he who offends one, possesses none and offends all; and every one [of them] confounds vices and sins. Holy wisdom confounds Satan and all his wickednesses. Pure holy simplicity confounds all the wisdom of this world and the wisdom of the flesh. Holy poverty confounds cupidity and avarice and the cares of this world. Holy humility confounds pride and all the men of this world and all things that are in the world. Holy charity confounds all diabolical and fleshly temptations and all fleshly fears. Holy obedience confounds all bodily and fleshly desires and keeps the body mortified to the obedience of the spirit and to the obedience of one's brother and makes a man subject to all the men of this world and not to men alone, but also to all beasts and wild animals, so that they may do with him whatsoever they will, in so far as it may be granted to them from above by the Lord.

St. Francis of Assisi.
Salutation of the Virtues.

Additional Biblical Reflections: 1 Corinthians 3:6–9; Philippians 4:8; 2 Peter 1:5–8.

Prayer

Lord, you are the fountain of virtue. Let us seek virtue not by our own accord but by receiving our virtues from your gracious hand. For virtue is a projection of you and your will, not us and our will. Couple the gift of virtue with gratitude so that they are not spoiled by pride and boasting but always testify to your grace and mercy. Amen.

DAY 5

The Lord's Prayer is arguably the most repeated prayer in Christendom. We pray it so regularly that the depth of its meaning might often be lost on our tongues. In today's meditation, St. Francis expands upon the Lord's Prayer by plumbing the depths of the prayer our Lord taught us.

Meditations from St. Francis

Our Father, most holy, our Creator, Redeemer, and Comforter.

Who art in heaven, in the angels and in the saints illuminating them unto knowledge, for Thou, O Lord, art light; inflaming them unto love, for Thou, O Lord, art Love; dwelling in them and filling them with blessedness, for Thou, O Lord, art the highest Good, the eternal Good from whom is all good and without whom is no good.

Hallowed be Thy Name: may Thy knowledge shine in us that we may know the breadth of Thy benefits, the length of Thy promises, the height of Thy majesty, and the depth of Thy judgments.

Thy Kingdom come, that Thou mayest reign in us by grace and mayest make us come to Thy Kingdom, where there is the clear vision of Thee, the perfect love of Thee, the blessed company of Thee, the eternal enjoyment of Thee.

Thy will be done on earth as it is in heaven, that we may love Thee with the whole heart by always thinking of Thee; with the whole soul by always desiring Thee; with the whole mind by directing all our intentions to Thee and seeking Thy honor in all things and with all our strength, by spending all the powers and senses of body and soul in the service of Thy love and not in anything else; and that we may love our neighbors even as ourselves, drawing to the best of our power all to Thy love; rejoicing in the good of others as in our own and compassionating [them] in troubles and giving offence to no one.

Give us this day, through memory and understanding and reverence for the love which He had for us and for those things which He said, did, and suffered, for us,—our daily bread, Thy Beloved Son, our Lord Jesus Christ.

And forgive us our trespasses, by Thy ineffable mercy in virtue of the Passion of Thy Beloved Son, our Lord Jesus Christ, and through the merits and intercession of the most Blessed Virgin Mary and of all Thy elect.

As we forgive their that trespass against us, and what we do not fully forgive, do Thou, O Lord, make us fully forgive, that for Thy sake we may truly love our enemies and devoutly intercede for them with Thee; that we may render no evil for evil, but in Thee may strive to do good to all.

And lead us not into temptation, hidden or visible, sudden or continuous. But deliver us from evil, past, present, and to come. Amen.

St. Francis of Assisi. The Praises.

Additional Biblical Reflections: Matthew 6:9–13; Luke 11:1–13; Philippians 4:6.

Prayer

Lord, you have given us a wealth of wisdom in the pattern by which you taught us to pray. Let us meditate on these words so that they are not hollow but genuine pleas that fulfill the request that thy will is done in our lives. Amen.

DAY 6

Creation itself testifies to God's glory. In today's meditation, St. Francis offers a canticle that praises the earth's elements for the ways they reflect God's goodness. One can appreciate the artist by beholding his art, the architect by wondering at his structures. Likewise, when we behold the elements of this world properly, they do not become false deities but evidences and glories of our Creator God.

Meditations from St. Francis

Most high, omnipotent, good Lord,
Praise, glory and honor and benediction all, are Thine.
To Thee alone do they belong, most High,
And there is no man fit to mention Thee.
Praise be to Thee, my Lord, with all Thy creatures,
Especially to my worshipful brother sun,
The which lights up the day, and through him dost Thou brightness give;
And beautiful is he and radiant with splendor great;
Of Thee, most High, signification gives.

Praised be my Lord, for sister moon and for the stars,
In heaven Thou hast formed them clear and precious and fair.

Praised be my Lord for brother wind

And for the air and clouds and fair and every kind of weather,
By the which Thou givest to Thy creatures nourishment.
Praised be my Lord for sister water,
The which is greatly helpful and humble and precious and pure.

Praised be my Lord for brother fire,
By the which Thou lightest up the dark.
And fair is he and gay and mighty and strong.

Praised be my Lord for our sister, mother earth,
The which sustains and keeps us
And brings forth diverse fruits with grass and flowers bright.

Praised be my Lord for those who for Thy love forgive
And weakness bear and tribulation.
Blessed those who shall in peace endure,
For by Thee, most High, shall they be crowned.
Praised be my Lord for our sister, the bodily death,
From the which no living man can flee.
Woe to them who die in mortal sin;
Blessed those who shall find themselves in Thy most holy will,
For the second death shall do them no ill.

Praise ye and bless ye my Lord, and give Him thanks,
And be subject unto Him with great humility.

St. Francis of Assisi. *The*
Canticle of the Sun.

Additional Biblical Reflections: Job 12:7; Romans 1:20; 2 Peter 3:10.

Prayer

Lord, throughout your Word, you reveal yourself to us through the elements of your creation. You guided Israel by a pillar of wind and fire. You brought your people through the water, even as you have brought us all through baptism. And your Spirit descended as tongues of fire. Even the wind and the sea obeyed your Word. Let us see, in all things, your mighty hand at work so that we might always revere your glory. Amen.

DAY 7

Even God's law, which is good and holy, kills when we esteem those words unto ourselves and use our obedience to those words as a cause to become puffed up in pride. While the letter does, indeed, kill, when taken alone—for us, whom the spirit has already quickened—the letter takes a new meaning, not a deadly burden but a joyful path of obedience and holiness.

Meditations from St. Francis

The Apostle says, "the letter killeth, but the spirit quickeneth." They are killed by the letter who seek only to know the words that they may be esteemed more learned among others and that they may acquire great riches to leave to their relations and friends. And those religious are killed by the letter who will not follow the spirit of the Holy Scriptures, but who seek rather to know the words only and to interpret them to others. And they are quickened by the spirit of the Holy Scriptures who do not interpret materially every text they know or wish to know, but who by word and example give them back to God from whom is all good.

St. Francis of Assisi.
*That Good Works Should
Accompany Knowledge.*

Additional Biblical Reflections: Psalm 19:7; John 6:63; 2 Corinthians 3:4–6.

Prayer

Lord, while the letter kills in your spirit, we have new life after the image of your son who died and rose. Grant, Lord, that we might always approach the letter not according to the flesh but the spirit so that we might learn from you all that is right and good. Amen.

DAY 8

Community has always been an important component of Christian living. As members of one body, if one member wanders, another might pull them back in line. Since we are all prone to wander and are easily tempted, the Lord has created holy communities of brothers and sisters who might hold us accountable. Here, we see that St. Francis did not believe that brothers should be admonished for the sake of some kind of purity or to protect the community, but out of love for the sake of the one who errs.

Meditations from St. Francis

Therefore take care of your souls and of those of your brothers, for "it is a fearful thing to fall into the hands of the living God." If however one of the ministers should command some one of the brothers anything contrary to our life or against his soul, the brother is not bound to obey him, because that is not obedience in which a fault or sin is committed. Nevertheless, let all the brothers who are subject to the ministers and servants consider reasonably and carefully the deeds of the ministers and servants. And if they should see any one of them walking according to the flesh and not according to the spirit, according to the right way of our life, after the third admonition, if he will not amend, let him be reported to the minister and servant of the whole fraternity in the Whitsun Chapter, in spite of any obstacle that may stand in the way. If however among the brothers, wherever they may be, there should be some brother who desires to live according to the flesh, and not according to the spirit, let the brothers with whom he is admonish, instruct, and correct him humbly and diligently. And if after the third admonition he will not amend, let them as soon as possible send him, or make the matter known to his minister and servant, and let the minister and servant do with him what may seem to him most expedient before God.

And let all the brothers, the ministers and servants as well as the others, take care not to be troubled or angered because of the fault or bad example of another, for the devil desires to corrupt many through the sin of one; but let them spiritually help him who has sinned, as best they can; for he that is whole needs not a physician, but he that is sick.

St. Francis of Assisi.
First Rule of the Friars Minor.

Additional Biblical Reflections: Proverbs 27:6; Luke 17:3; Colossians 3:16.

Prayer

Lord, thank you for calling us into your Church. These holy communities are meant not to force conformity but to ensure that all of us remain on the right path toward you. Let us hear our fellows' admonitions in such a way, and rather than taking offense, be grateful for the correction. Amen.

DAY 9

M uch has been written in recent years on the topic of servant leadership. This idea, now peddled regularly in business schools, is actually ancient wisdom. Here, St. Francis picks up on this idea concerning the friars. But even St. Francis did not invent this idea—he rightly points out that this way of leading "from below" was typified by Jesus, who humbled himself so that he might become the Lord of all by being the servant of all.

Meditations from St. Francis

In like manner let not all the brothers have power and authority, especially among themselves, for as the Lord says in the Gospel: "The princes of the Gentiles lord it over them: and they that are the greater exercise power upon them." It shall not be thus among the brothers, but whosoever will be the greater among them, let him be their minister and servant, and he that is the greater among them let him be as the younger, and he who is the first, let him be as the last. Let not any brother do evil or speak evil to another; let them rather in the spirit of charity willingly serve and obey each other: and this is the true and holy obedience of our Lord Jesus Christ. And let all the brothers as often soever as they may have declined from the commandments of God, and wandered from obedience, know that, as the prophet says, they are cursed out of obedience as long as they continue consciously in such a sin. And when they persevere in the commandments of the Lord, which they have promised by the holy Gospel and their life, let them know that they abide in true obedience, and are blessed by God.

St. Francis of Assisi.
First Rule of the Friars Minor.

Additional Biblical Reflections: Matthew 20:20-28; John 13:1–17; Philippians 2:3.

Prayer

Lord, though you were Lord of all, you made yourself our servant so we might be elevated to your place of glory. Grant us, Lord, servant hearts so that through our obedience, others might also see your glory. In Jesus's name. Amen.

DAY 10

Franciscans have been known, after St. Francis, for their renunciation of material things and vows of poverty. While not all people are given such a righteous name, it is not poverty alone that engenders holiness in these monastic communities. Rather, it's a removal of other things represented by material wealth that we readily turn into "gods" in our lives.

Meditations from St. Francis

The Lord commands in the Gospel: "Take heed, beware of all malice and avarice and guard yourselves from the solicitudes of this world, and the cares of this life." Therefore, let none of the brothers, wherever he may be or whithersoever he may go, carry or receive money or coin in any manner, or cause it to be received, either for clothing, or for books, or as the price of any labor, or indeed for any reason, except on account of the manifest necessity of the sick brothers. For we ought not to have more use and esteem of money and coin than of stones. And the devil seeks to blind those who desire or value it more than stones. Let us therefore take care lest after having left all things we lose the kingdom of heaven for such a trifle. And if we should chance to find money in any place, let us no more regard it than the dust we tread under our feet, for it is "vanity of vanities, and all is vanity." And if perchance, which God forbid, it should happen that any brother should collect or have money or coin, except only because of the aforesaid necessity of the sick, let all the brothers hold him for a false brother, a thief, a robber, and one having a purse, unless he should become truly penitent. And let the brothers in nowise receive money for alms or cause it to be received, seek it or cause it to be sought, or money for other houses or places; nor let them go with any person seeking money or coin for such places. But the brothers may perform all other services which are not contrary to our life, with the blessing of God. The brothers may however for the manifest necessity of the lepers ask alms for them But let them be very wary of money. But let all the brothers likewise take great heed not to search the world for any filthy lucre.

St. Francis of Assisi,
*First Rule of the Friars
Minor.*

Additional Biblical Reflections: Ecclesiastes 5:10; 1 Timothy 6:10; Hebrews 13:5.

Prayer

Lord, while money is not evil unto itself, the love of money can lead us down many perilous paths. Spare us from the love of material wealth so that our hearts might be fully devoted to you. In Jesus's name. Amen.

DAY 11

Community is there for more than to admonish. Our fellow believers are called to support one another in all affairs. If one is suffering, we suffer together. If one is hurting, we all hurt. If one is in need, the need is one we share and must work together to meet. In today's meditation, St. Francis encourages the friars to be aware of all the brothers' needs so that the community might meet whatever is required.

Meditations from St. Francis

If any of the brothers fall into sickness, wherever he may be, let the others not leave him, unless one of the brothers, or more if it be necessary, be appointed to serve him as they would wish to be served themselves; but in urgent necessity they may commit him to some person who will take care of him in his infirmity. And I ask the sick brother that he give thanks to the Creator for all things, and that he desire to be as God wills him to be, whether sick or well; for all whom the Lord has predestined to eternal life 1 are disciplined by the rod of afflictions and infirmities, and the spirit of compunction; as the Lord says: "Such as I love I rebuke and chastise." If, however, he be disquieted and angry, either against God or against the brothers, or perhaps ask eagerly for remedies, desiring too much to deliver his body which is soon to die, which is an enemy to the soul, this comes to him from evil and he is fleshly, and seems not to be of the brothers, because he loves his body more than his soul.

St. Francis of Assisi,
*First Rule of the Friars
Minor.*

Additional Biblical Reflections: Ecclesiastes 4:9–12; Hebrews 10:24–25; Romans 12:3–33.

Prayer

Lord, give us open eyes and ears to see the needs of our fellow believers, for we are your hands and mouthpiece, the touch that heals and the voice that restores. In this way, might all your Church be built up so that we might persist through this life until life everlasting. Amen.

DAY 12

Debate and dispute can be addictive. Lovers of controversy often seek it. They might even get a thrill from it. But it can also be damaging and destructive, particularly in the church. Rather, as God's people, St. Francis reminds us that we are to love one another and love peace rather than discord.

Meditations from St. Francis

And let all the brothers take care not to calumniate anyone, nor to contend in words; let them indeed study to maintain silence as far as God gives them grace. Let them also not dispute among themselves or with others, but let them be ready to answer with humility, saying: "we are unprofitable servants." And let them not be angry, for "whosoever is angry with his brother shall be in danger of the judgment. And whosoever shall say to his brother, Raca, shall be in danger of the council. And whosoever shall say, Thou fool, shall be in danger of hell fire." And let them love one another, as the Lord says: "This is My commandment, that you love one another, as I have loved you." And let them show their love by the works they do for each other, according as the Apostle says: "let us not love in word or in tongue, but in deed and in truth." Let them "speak evil of no man," nor murmur, nor detract others, for it is written: "Whisperers and detractors are hateful to God." And let them be "gentle, showing all mildness toward all men." Let them not judge and not condemn, and, as the Lord says, let them not pay attention to the least sins of others, but rather let them recount their own in the bitterness of their soul. And let them "strive to enter by the narrow gate," for the Lord says: "How narrow is the gate, and strait is the way that leadeth to life, and few there are that find it!"

St. Francis of Assisi,
*First Rule of the Friars
Minor.*

Additional Biblical Reflections: Proverbs 18:17–18; 2 Timothy 3:9–11; Titus 3:9–11.

Prayer

Lord, there can be no division in your body. You have called us to pursue your truth in harmony and peace, to love you as one body, and to love one another in kind. Grant us spirits of peace and understanding so that we might always strive to grow closer to you as one people, one body. Amen.

DAY 13

Sin usually creeps in through seemingly innocent actions. Appreciation for beauty can turn into lust. Appreciation for a brother's accomplishment can turn into envy. Associating with the ungodly, out of a desire to share God's truth with them, can also impact us to follow them instead if we are not careful. In today's meditation, St. Francis takes seriously the impressions we give and the dangers we carelessly expose ourselves to so that we might act wisely.

Meditations from St. Francis

Let all the brothers, wherever they are or may go, carefully avoid unbecoming looks, and company of women, and let no one converse with them alone. Let the priests speak to them honestly, giving them penance or some spiritual counsel. And let no woman whatsoever be received to obedience by any brother, but spiritual counsel being given to her let her do penance where she wills. Let us all carefully watch over ourselves, and hold all our members in subjection, for the Lord says: "Whosoever shall look on a woman to lust after her, hath already committed adultery with her in his heart."

St. Francis of Assisi,
*First Rule of the Friars
Minor.*

Additional Biblical Reflections: Malachi 2:7; Romans 14:13–23; 1 Corinthians 8:9.

Prayer

Lord, you have called us to be a light unto the world. We are meant to demonstrate your love to others. Therefore, ensure that we embrace your ways in all we do and say so that we not become a scandal but might always be your vessels in service to your glory. Amen.

DAY 14

As St. Francis exhorted his friars to travel from place to place, his words are reminiscent of the time that Jesus sent out 72 disciples to proclaim His message and prepare His way. In every instance, what rings true is an eternal kingdom perspective. They were to go forth in faith—depending on others' generosity—and willingly take any manner of persecution without retaliation. All of this was meant to show that the cares of this world mean little compared to the eternal message they were spreading.

Meditations from St. Francis

When the brothers travel through the world, let them carry nothing by the way, neither bag, nor purse, nor bread, nor money, nor a staff. And whatsoever house they shall enter, let them first say, "Peace be to this house," and remaining in the same house, let them eat and drink what things they have. Let them not resist evil, but if anyone should strike them on the cheek, let them turn to him the other; and if anyone take away their garment, let them not forbid him the tunic also. Let them give to everyone that asketh them, and if anyone take away their goods, let them not ask them again.

St. Francis of Assisi,
*First Rule of the Friars
Minor.*

Additional Biblical Reflections: Matthew 5:28–40; Luke 10:1–23; 1 Peter 4:12–14.

Prayer

Lord, you have sent us into the world not to be consumed by the cares of this world but with a message of your kingdom. Let all we do, and the way we carry ourselves, manifest this eternal perspective so that the truth of your message might shine through the darkness of the world. Amen.

DAY 15

Today's meditation picks up on yesterday's theme. When God sends us out, He does not do so in the ways that the world would expect. He does not send His Church into the world with power and might, but with humility and charity. While it is counterintuitive, when viewed from the perspective of faith, it makes sense. For even if the wolves devour the sheep, in faith, we know that God can and will raise up His sheep again.

Meditations from St. Francis

The Lord says: "Behold, I send you as sheep in the midst of wolves. Be ye therefore wise as serpents and simple as doves." Wherefore, whoever of the brothers may wish, by divine inspiration, to go among the Saracens and other infidels, let them go with the permission of their minister and servant. But let the minister give them leave and not refuse them, if he sees they are fit to be sent; he will be held to render an account to the Lord if in this or in other things he acts indiscreetly. The brothers, however, who go may conduct themselves in two ways spiritually among them. One way is not to make disputes or contentions; but let them be "subject to every human creature for God's sake," yet confessing themselves to be Christians. The other way is that when they see it is pleasing to God, they announce the Word of God, that they may believe in Almighty God,—Father, and Son, and Holy Ghost, the Creator of all, our Lord the Redeemer and Saviour the Son, and that they should be baptized and be made Christians, because, "unless a man be born again of water and the Holy Ghost, he cannot enter into the kingdom of God." These and other things which please God they may say to them, for the Lord says in the Gospel: "Everyone that shall confess Me before men, I will also confess him before My Father who is in heaven;" and "he that shall be ashamed of Me and My words, of him the Son of Man shall be ashamed, when He shall come in His majesty and that of His Father, and of the holy angels."

St. Francis of Assisi,
*First Rule of the Friars
Minor.*

Additional Biblical Reflections: Isaiah 53:7–9; Matthew 10:16–33; Revelation 5:6.

Prayer

Lord, while you send us out as sheep amongst wolves, you were the lamb who was sent to take away the sin of the world. Let us go forth in confidence, for the lamb that was slain has arisen again. In Jesus's name. Amen.

DAY 16

According to St. Francis, citing the Bible in several places, even our bodies are not our own. For this reason, to offer our bodies in service to the Kingdom of God is not only reasonable but expected. Once again, we are reminded that an eternal perspective, rather than a temporal one, alters how we live our lives. What might we do differently, today, if we set aside temporary concerns and were focused on our heavenly goal?

Meditations from St. Francis

And let all the brothers, wherever they may be, remember that they have given themselves, and have relinquished their bodies to our Lord Jesus Christ; and for love of Him they ought to expose themselves to enemies both visible and invisible, for the Lord says: "Whosoever shall lose his life for My sake, shall save it" in eternal life. "Blessed are they that suffer persecution for justice' sake, for theirs is the kingdom of heaven." "If they have persecuted Me, they will also persecute you." If however they should persecute you in one city, flee to another. "Blessed are ye when they shall revile you, and persecute you, and speak all that is evil against you, untruly, for My sake." "Be glad in that day and rejoice, for your reward is great in heaven." "I say to you, my friends, be not afraid of them who kill the body, and after that have no more that they can do." "See that ye are not troubled." "In your patience you shall possess your souls." "But he that shall persevere unto the end, he shall be saved."

St. Francis of Assisi,
*First Rule of the Friars
Minor.*

Additional Biblical Reflections: Matthew 16:25; Mark 8:35; Luke 12:4.

Prayer

Dear Lord, you have given us our bodies, eyes, and ears—all our senses. However, our bodies, given from you, still belong to you. Thus, allow us to learn to live sacrificially, dedicating our bodily lives to your service and glory so that your name might be glorified, and we might achieve our heavenly goal. In Jesus's name. Amen.

DAY 17

The Lord has called us to confess our sins to one another. When we bring what is in the darkness into the light, it loses its power. Thus, confessing our sins is not only advised so that we might be forgiven and receive grace but so the sin itself would not fester in our souls and lead to further transgressions.

Meditations from St. Francis

Let my blessed brothers, both clerics and laics, confess their sins to priests of our religion. And if they cannot do this, let them confess to other discreet and Catholic priests, knowing firmly and hoping that from whatever Catholic priests they may receive penance and absolution, they will undoubtedly be absolved from these sins if they take care to observe humbly and faithfully the penance enjoined them. If however they cannot then have a priest, let them confess to their brother, as the Apostle James says: "Confess your sins to one another;" 1 but let them not on this account fail to have recourse to priests, for to priests alone the power of binding and loosing has been given. And thus contrite and having confessed, let them receive the Body and Blood of our Lord Jesus Christ with great humility and veneration, calling to mind what the Lord Himself says: "He that eateth

My Flesh and drinketh My Blood hath everlasting life," and "Do this for a commemoration of Me."

St. Francis of Assisi,
*First Rule of the Friars
Minor.*

Additional Biblical Reflections: John 6:54–56; James 5:16; 1 John 1:9–14.

Prayer

Lord, grant us the courage to confess our sins to one another. By doing so, may our hearts be purified, and our souls redeemed from transgression. Bring what festers in the darkness into the light so that we might be drawn to you. Amen.

DAY 18

We are often told to follow our hearts. However, we hear, as St. Francis reminds us, in the scriptures that out of the hearts of men proceed wickedness and all kinds of vice. Rather than following our hearts, we must submit our hearts to Jesus Christ. For what is evil comes from the heart of men. What is good and salutary comes from the heart of our Lord.

Meditations from St. Francis

Let us all, brothers, give heed to what the Lord says: "Love your enemies, and do good to them that hate you." For our Lord Jesus, whose footsteps we ought to follow, called His betrayer friend, and offered Himself willingly to His crucifiers. Therefore all those who unjustly inflict upon us tribulations and anguishes, shames and injuries, sorrows and torments, martyrdom and death, are our friends whom we ought to love much, because we gain eternal life by that which they make us suffer. And let us hate our body with its vices and sins, because by living carnally it wishes to deprive us of the love of our Lord Jesus Christ and eternal life, and to lose itself with all else in hell; for we by our own fault are corrupt, miserable, and averse to good, but prompt and willing to evil; because, as the Lord says in the Gospel: from the heart of men proceed and come evil thoughts, adulteries, fornications, murders, thefts, covetousness, wickedness, deceit, lasciviousness, an evil eye, false testimonies, blasphemy, foolishness. All these evils come from within, from the heart of man, and these are what defile a man.

St. Francis of Assisi,
First Rule of the Friars
Minor.

Additional Biblical Reflections: Ezekiel 28:17; Matthew 15:18–20; Mark 7:20–23.

Prayer

Lord, you made our hearts good. But now, consumed by sin, our hearts produce all kinds of vice. Create in us clean hearts so that we might be redeemed and exemplars of your love and mercy. In Jesus's name. Amen.

DAY 19

According to St. Francis, the reason for renouncing the world is not so much because they world itself is evil—God created the world and declared it good—but because this world is corrupt, and a new heaven and earth is on the way. Thus, renouncing the world, we are prepared to follow God's will and act in ways that please Him.

Meditations from St. Francis

But now, after having renounced the world, we have nothing else to do but to be solicitous, to follow the will of God, and to please Him. Let us take much care that we be not the wayside, or the stony or thorny ground, according to what the Lord says in the Gospel: The seed is the word of God. And that which fell by the wayside and was trampled under foot are they that hear the word and do not understand, then the devil cometh, and snatcheth that which has been sown in their hearts and taketh the word out of their hearts, lest believing they should be saved. But that which fell upon the rock are they who, when they hear the word, at once receive it with joy; but when tribulation and persecution arise on account of the word, they are immediately scandalized, and these have no roots in themselves, but are for a while, for they believe for a while, and in time of temptation fall away But that which fell among thorns are they who hear the word of God, and the solicitude and cares of this world, the fallacies of riches, and the desire of other things entering in choke the word, and it becomes unfruitful. But that sown on good ground are they who, in a good and best heart, hearing the word understand and keep it, and bring forth fruit in patience. And for this reason, brothers, let us, as the Lord says, "let the dead bury their dead." And let us be much on our guard against the malice and cunning of Satan, who desires that man should not give his heart and mind to the Lord God, and who going about seeks to seduce the heart of man under pretext of some reward or benefit, to smother the words and precepts of the Lord from memory, and who wishes to blind the heart of man by worldly business and cares, and to dwell there, as the Lord says: "When an unclean spirit is gone out of a man, he walketh through dry places seeking rest and findeth none; then he saith: 'I will return into my house whence I came out.' And coming he findeth it empty, swept, and garnished. Then he goeth and taketh with him seven other spirits more wicked than himself, and they enter in, and dwell there; and the last state of that man is made worse than the first." 1 Wherefore let us all, brothers, watch much, lest under pretext of some reward or labor or aid we lose or separate our mind and heart from the Lord. But I beseech all the brothers, both the ministers and others, in the charity which God is, 2 that, overcoming all obstacles and putting aside all care and solicitude, they strive in the best manner they are able, to serve, love, and honor the Lord God with a clean heart and a pure mind, which He seeks above all.

St. Francis of Assisi,
*First Rule of the Friars
Minor.*

Additional Biblical Reflections: Luke 16:33; 1 Peter 4:7; Revelation 13:1–18.

Prayer

Lord, this world is full of many things that can sway our hearts. Grant us a holy focus and resolve to follow your will and keep material things in perspective. For, while you grant us everything in the world, these things are not ends unto themselves but tokens of your love. In Jesus's name. Amen.

DAY 20

Doctrine is more than dogma. It is life. Unlike the Pharisees, who missed the forest for the trees, the teaching of the Scriptures is meant to manifest His name and reveal His glory. As we face the cares of this world, the teaching of Christ is like a tether that ties us to our eternal destination. St. Francis urges us to retain this perspective as we seek His truth in His word.

Meditations from St. Francis

Let us therefore hold fast the words, the life and doctrine and holy Gospel of Him who deigned for us to ask His Father to manifest to us His Name, saying: Father, I have manifested Thy Name to the men whom Thou hast given Me because the words which Thou gavest Me I have given to them, and they have received them, and have known in very deed that I came forth out of Thee, and they have believed that Thou didst send Me. I pray for them, I pray not for the world, but for them whom Thou hast given Me, because they are Thine and all My things are Thine. Holy Father, keep them in Thy Name whom Thou hast given Me, that they may be one, as We also are. These things I speak in the world that they may have joy filled in themselves. I have given them Thy word, and the world hath hated them, because they are not of the world, as I also am not of the world. I pray not that Thou shouldst take them out of the world, but that Thou shouldst keep them from evil. Sanctify them in truth. Thy word is truth As Thou hast sent Me into the world, I have sent them into the world. And for them I do sanctify Myself, that they may be sanctified in truth. Not for them only do I pray, but for them also who through their word shall believe in Me, that they may be consummated in one, and that the world may know that Thou hast sent Me, and hast loved them, as Thou hast also loved Me. And I have made known Thy Name to them, that the love wherewith Thou hast loved Me may be in them, and I in them. Father, I will that where I am, they also whom Thou hast given Me may be with Me, that they may see Thy glory in Thy kingdom.

St. Francis of Assisi,
*First Rule of the Friars
Minor.*

Additional Biblical Reflections: Ephesians 4:14; Titus 1:9–2:1; Hebrews 13:9.

Prayer

Lord, your word is more than pure thinking; it is a light that illuminates our path. Guide us through your Spirit so that we might glean your will from your word and always pursue your truth in ways that illuminate your kingdom. Amen.

DAY 21

St. Francis did not view his role and authority as a position of power but one whereby he could serve others. By that, he urges others to follow the example of Christ, who likewise viewed himself not according to the majesty and reverence he was owed but as a servant who offered himself to others out of love.

Meditations from St. Francis

To all Christians, religious, clerics, and laics, men and women, to all who dwell in the whole world, Brother Francis, their servant and subject, presents reverent homage, wishing true peace from heaven and sincere charity in the Lord. Being the servant of all, I am bound to serve all and to administer the balm-bearing words of my Lord. Wherefore, considering in my mind that, because of the infirmity and weakness of my body, I cannot visit each one personally, I propose by this present letter and message to offer you the words of our Lord Jesus Christ who is the Word of the Father and the words of the Holy Ghost which are "spirit and life" This Word of the Father, so worthy, so holy and glorious, whose coming the most High Father announced from heaven by His holy archangel Gabriel to the holy and glorious Virgin Mary in whose womb He received the true flesh of our humanity and frailty, He, being rich above all, willed, nevertheless, with His most Blessed Mother, to choose poverty.

St. Francis of Assisi,
Letter to All the Faithful.

Additional Biblical Reflections: Mark 10:45; Galatians 5:13; 1 Peter 4:9–19.

Prayer

Lord, you are worthy of all honor and praise. But when you came to our world, you came in the form of a servant, so we, who follow you, might likewise become servants to others. Let us have servant hearts so that your life might flow through us in the care for others. Amen.

DAY 22

S t. Francis frequently wrote about the Eucharist—particularly because the sacrament illuminates what he believed to be the heart of the faith, that is, the cross of Christ. It is easy to be distracted by discipline, piety, even church activities and functions. However, we must never forget that the cross is at the intersection between this life and life everlasting. More than that, the cross redefines what this very life means. Freed from sin, we can live differently.

Meditations from St. Francis

And when His Passion was nigh, He celebrated the Pasch with His disciples and, taking bread, He gave thanks and blessed and broke saying: Take ye and eat: this is My Body. And, taking the chalice, He said: This is My Blood of the New Testament, which shall be shed for you and for many unto remission of sins. After that He prayed to the Father, saying: "Father, if it be possible, let this chalice pass from Me." "And His sweat became as drops of blood, trickling down upon the ground." But withal, He gave up His will to the will of the Father, saying: Father, Thy will be done: not as I will, but as Thou wilt. Such was the will of the Father that His Son, Blessed and Glorious, whom He gave to us, and who was born for us, should by His own Blood, sacrifice, and oblation, offer Himself on the altar of the Cross, not for Himself, by whom "all things were made," but for our sins, leaving us an example that we should follow His steps. And He wishes that we should all be saved by Him and that we should receive Him with a pure heart and a chaste body. But there are few who wish to receive Him and to be saved by Him, although His yoke is sweet and His burden light.

St. Francis of Assisi,
Letter to All the Faithful.

Additional Biblical Reflections: Galatians 2:20; 1 Corinthians 1:18–24; Philippians 2:8.

Prayer

Lord, while the cross is the last thing anyone expected might manifest your glory, for us, who are baptized into your name, it is no longer a cursed tree but one that bears life-giving fruit. Grant that we would all live cruciform lives as living sacrifices, who rest in your grace and forgiveness, and with gratitude, live differently as we await the consummation of what you achieved for us at Calvary. Amen.

DAY 23

For St. Francis, the Mass was not only central to Christian piety and worship but at the heart of a Christian's life. That is because, in the mass, one finds the forgiveness of sins, a pattern for life, and the strength to live in abstention from sin and vice. This is why, according to St. Francis, the "religious" are not merely those who fast for fasting's sake but do all such things in order so that they might do "more and greater things."

Meditations from St. Francis

We ought also to fast and to abstain from vices and sins and from superfluity of food and drink, and to be Catholics. We ought also to visit Churches frequently and to reverence clerics not only for themselves, if they are sinners, but on account of their office and administration of the most holy Body and Blood of our Lord Jesus Christ, which they sacrifice on the altar and receive and administer to others. And let us all know for certain that no one can be saved except by the Blood of our Lord Jesus Christ and by the holy words of the Lord which clerics say and announce and distribute and they alone administer and not others. But religious especially, who have renounced the world, are bound to do more and greater things, but "not to leave the other undone."

St. Francis of Assisi,
Letter to All the Faithful.

Additional Biblical Reflections: John 1:29; 2 Corinthians 12:9; Hebrews 7:27.

Prayer

Lord, you have not given us rites, rituals, or laws merely so that we might prove ourselves obedient. Rather, you've given us such things so we might come into contact with you, on account of the cross of Christ. May your body and blood nourish us, grant us your grace, and sustain us until the final feast might be enjoyed in your heavenly kingdom. Amen.

DAY 24

Once again, in today's meditation, St. Francis reminds us to be wary of our bodies and urges. Many people in the world will tell us to follow our emotions and whatever we desire. Ancient philosophies rooted in the pursuit of pleasure continue to reemerge in pop philosophy and culture. But what we are called to is a life that is not controlled by the body but *in* the body that is brought into obedience under the cross's image.

Meditations from St. Francis

We ought to hate our bodies with [their] vices and sins, because the Lord says in the Gospel that all vices and sins come forth from the heart. We ought to love our enemies and do good to them that hate us. We ought to observe the precepts and counsels of our Lord Jesus Christ. We ought also to deny ourselves and to put our bodies beneath the yoke of servitude and holy obedience as each one has promised to the Lord. And let no man be bound by obedience to obey any one in that where sin or offence is committed. But let him to whom obedience has been entrusted and who is considered greater become as the lesser and the servant of the other brothers, and let him show and have the mercy toward each of his brothers that he would wish to be shown to himself if he were in the like situation. And let him not be angry with a brother on account of his offence, but let him advise him kindly and encourage him with all patience and humility.

St. Francis of Assisi,
Letter to All the Faithful.

Additional Biblical Reflections: Romans 8:5; Galatians 5:19–21; Colossians 3:1–25.

Prayer

Lord, all things that come from you are good. The same is true of our bodies. Nonetheless, sin is often the result of the misuse of good things—our bodies, desires, thoughts, and the like. Discipline us in the flesh, Lord, so that our bodies might be slaves of righteousness and we might remain free in your Spirit. Amen.

DAY 25

Today's meditation continues to reflect on the relationship between our bodies and the spiritual life. However, St. Francis's advice has more to do with individual piety, but it also impacts how we view ourselves concerning others. For we are not isolated "temples" of the Holy Spirit, but a unified temple, a Church, whom Christ has declared His singular bride.

Meditations from St. Francis

We ought not to be "wise according to the flesh" and prudent, but we ought rather to be simple, humble, and pure. And let us hold our bodies in dishonor and contempt because through our fault we are all wretched and corrupt, foul and worms, as the Lord says by the prophet: "I am a worm and no man, the reproach of men and the outcast of the people." We should never desire to be above others, but ought rather to be servants and subject "to every human creature for God's sake." And the spirit of the Lord shall rest upon all those who do these things and who shall persevere to the end, and He shall make His abode and dwelling in them, and they shall be children of the heavenly Father whose works they do, and they are the spouses, brothers and mothers of our Lord Jesus Christ. We are spouses when by the Holy Ghost the faithful soul is united to Jesus Christ. We are His brothers when we do the will of His Father who is in heaven. We are His mothers when we bear Him in our heart and in our body through pure love and a clean conscience and we bring Him forth by holy work which ought to shine as an example to others.

St. Francis of Assisi,
Letter to All the Faithful.

Additional Biblical Reflections: Isaiah 61:10; Mark 2:19–20; Revelation 19:9.

Prayer

Lord, you are the source of all wisdom. When we seek wisdom in the flesh, we pile folly upon folly. But in you, we find in the apparent foolishness of the cross great insights that defy human reason but offer eternal life and a path of righteousness. Grant us, Lord, full trust in your ways so that we might seek wisdom only in you. Amen.

DAY 26

In today's meditation, we hear how Jesus intercedes on our behalf so that His might is also ours. For what was once ours—our sin—He accepted in His flesh when He went to the cross. We do well to ponder St. Francis's exuberance for these things. So often, when we hear of these things, we forget how profound and astounding they truly are. We would do well, with St. Francis, to recapture our marvel and wonder at what our Lord did for us.

Meditations from St. Francis

O how glorious and holy and great to have a Father in heaven! O how holy, fair, and lovable to have a spouse in heaven! O how holy and how beloved, well pleasing and humble, peaceful and sweet and desirable above all to have such a brother who has laid down His life for His sheep, and who has prayed for us to the Father, saying: Father, keep them in Thy Name whom Thou hast given Me. Father, all those whom Thou hast given Me in the world were Thine, and Thou hast given them to Me. And the words which Thou gavest Me I have given to them; and they have received them, and have known in very deed that I came forth from Thee, and they have believed that Thou didst send Me. I pray for them: not for the world: bless and sanctify them. And for them I sanctify Myself that they may be sanctified in one as We also are. And I will, Father, that where I am, they also may be with Me, that they may see My glory in My kingdom. And since

He has suffered so many things for us and has done and will do so much good to us, let every creature which is in heaven and on earth and in the sea and in the abysses render praise to God and glory and honor and benediction; for He is our strength and power who alone is good, alone most high, alone almighty and admirable, glorious and alone holy, praiseworthy and blessed without end forever and ever. Amen.

St. Francis of Assisi,
Letter to All the Faithful.

Additional Biblical Reflections: Hosea 11:1; John 17:1–26; Ephesians 1:13–14.

Prayer

Dearest Lord, while we were still sinners, you took our place so that we might also take your place in Heaven—even as we go to our death, in you, so, too, do we go to life everlasting with you at the right hand of God. Grant us consolation in knowing these things, so we might live lives worthy of the calling we have received and be sanctified in your image. Amen.

DAY 27

St. Francis says the whole world should tremble at God Almighty, who comes to an altar in the hands of a priest. Yet, St. Francis also cites this as a reason to praise. How different God's presence is for those who do not know Him—who do not take hold of the benefits of Christ—compared to those who do. For God Almighty is still God Almighty. To many, His presence is at error. But for those of us whom He calls His children, it is the greatest possible comfort.

Meditations from St. Francis

Consider your dignity, brothers, priests, and be holy because He Himself is holy. And as the Lord God has honored you above all through this mystery, even so do you also love and reverence and honor Him above all. It is a great misery and a deplorable weakness when you have Him thus present to care for anything else in the whole world. Let the entire man be seized with fear; let the whole world tremble; let heaven exult when Christ, the Son of the Living God, is on the altar in the hands of the priest. O admirable height and stupendous condescension! O humble sublimity! O sublime humility! that the Lord of the universe, God and the Son of God, so humbles Himself that for our salvation He hides Himself under a morsel of bread. Consider, brothers, the humility of God and "pour out your hearts before Him," and be ye humbled that ye may be exalted by

Him. Do not therefore keep back anything for yourselves that He may receive you entirely who gives Himself up entirely to you.

Francis of Assisi, *To All the Friars.*

Additional Biblical Reflections: Psalm 111:10; Proverbs 8:13; Matthew 10:28.

Prayer

Lord, no one has descended further or from greater heights to such low lows than you from the throne of Heaven to a human birth and a death reserved for criminals. However, you have comprehended all things, and your redemption covers us no matter our status in life. Grant that we might always have a healthy fear of your majesty and constant solace on account of your grace. Amen.

DAY 28

How easy is it to fall into complacency for holy things. We have attended many masses, received the Sacrament more times than we can count, and find ourselves with wandering minds, going through the motions, without the sense of awe these things demand. St. Francis reminds us of the wonder of these things, so they do not become mundane but that we always hold them in their proper reference.

Meditations from St. Francis

Consider your dignity, brothers, priests, and be holy because He Himself is holy. And as the Lord God has honored you above all through this mystery, even so do you also love and reverence and honor Him above all. It is a great misery and a deplorable weakness when you have Him thus present to care for anything else in the whole world. Let the entire man be seized with fear; let the whole world tremble; let heaven exult when Christ, the Son of the Living God, is on the altar in the hands of the priest. O admirable height and stupendous condescension! O humble sublimity! O sublime humility! that the Lord of the universe, God and the Son of God, so humbles Himself that for our salvation He hides Himself under a morsel of bread.

Francis of Assisi, *To All the Friars.*

Additional Biblical Reflections: Amos 6:1; John 1:1–3; 1 Timothy 3:16.

Prayer

Lord, you exhibit not only the greatest majesty but the most profound humility. Yet, you are without arrogance or pride. Let us, likewise, find glory in your gifts without being prideful or boastful. In these things, let your glory leave us in constant awe so that we might not become complacent in our piety. In Jesus's name. Amen.

DAY 29

Our faith is not dependent on others. While we should love even the noblest and most pious of our spiritual mentors, as we are called to love all men, they should never eclipse our love of God. For if we hinge our faith on human beings, when they fail, as humans are prone to do, our faith will fail with them. However, when we love others through the heart of Christ, our faith will never falter.

Meditations from St. Francis

I speak to thee as best I can on the subject of thy soul; that those things which impede thee in loving the Lord God and whosoever may be a hindrance to thee, whether brothers or others, even though they were to strike thee—all these things thou oughtest to reckon as a favor And so thou shouldst desire and not otherwise. And let this be to thee for true obedience from the Lord God and from me, for this I know surely to be true obedience. And love those that do such things to thee and wish not other from them, save in so far as the Lord may grant to thee; and in this thing love them—by wishing that they may be better Christians. And let this be to thee more than a hermitage. And by this I wish to know if thou lovest God and me His servant and thine, to wit: that there be no brother in the world who has sinned, how great soever his sin may be, who after he has seen thy face shall ever go away without thy mercy, if he seek mercy, and, if he seek not mercy, ask thou him if he desires mercy. And if he afterwards appears before thy face a thousand times, love him more than me, to the end that thou mayest draw him to the Lord, and on such ones always have mercy And this thou shouldst declare to the guardians, when thou canst, that thou art determined of thyself to do thus.

St. Francis of Assisi. *To a Certain Minister.*

Additional Biblical Reflections: Luke 14:26; Colossians 3:1–2; Romans 12:2.

Prayer

Lord, you are the highest object of our hearts. May our love of others always be an extension of our love of you and your love for us and all people. In this way, Lord, strengthen our faith so that we might endure no matter what others might do and remain faithful to you in all things. Amen.

DAY 30

It may be tempting to ask whether some of the practices and traditions we exercise in our reverence of God, and the Eucharist, are necessary. Indeed, not all traditions that demonstrate such reverence have persisted throughout history. Nonetheless, we must maintain reverence and awe for what meets the eye—bread and wine, and even the priest are common in every respect. However, according to God's Word, what is truly occurring is the greatest and most profound mystery: An encounter with the Divine.

Meditations from St. Francis

I entreat you more than if it were a question of myself that, when it is becoming and it may seem to be expedient, you humbly beseech the clerics to venerate above all the most holy Body and Blood of our Lord Jesus Christ and His Holy Name and written words which sanctify the body. They ought to hold as precious the chalices, corporals, ornaments of the altar, and all that pertain to the Sacrifice And if the most holy Body of the Lord be lodged very poorly in any place, let It according to the command of the Church be placed by them and left in a precious place, and let It be carried with great veneration and administered to others with discretion. The Names also and written words of the Lord, wheresoever they may be found in unclean places, let them be collected, and they ought to be put in a proper place. And in all the preaching you do, admonish the people concerning penance and that no one can be saved except he that receives the most sacred Body and Blood of the Lord. And while It is being sacrificed by the priest on the altar and It is being carried to any place, let all the people on bended knees render praise, honor, and glory to the Lord God Living and True. And you shall so announce and preach His praise to all peoples that at every hour and when the bells are rung praise and thanks shall always be given to the Almighty God by all the people through the whole earth.

St. Francis of Assisi. *To All the Custodes.*

Additional Biblical Reflections: Leviticus 26:2; Luke 12:5; Hebrews 12:18–29.

Prayer

Lord, not all your mysteries can be investigated, but all of them should be revered. Let us guard our practice and actions so that all we do maintains a posture of reverence that recognizes your presence and majesty. May all these things constantly arrest our hearts so we might ever be mindful of you and your will. Amen.